CHINESE FESTIVALS

Chinese New Year

Edited by Li Chaodong
Translated by Joanna Jiayan Zhang and Vivian Qinwen Yan

Books Beyond Boundaries
ROYAL COLLINS

According to legend, in ancient China, there was a kind of monster called "Nian." It had horns on its head and was very fierce. Usually, the beast Nian hid in the mountains. On every Chinese New Year's Eve, the beast Nian would go down the mountain to the village to eat livestock and even people.

The beast Nian was most afraid of red, fire, and noise. So, on Chinese New Year's Eve, the villagers put on red clothes, lit red candles in the house, pasted red paper on the door, and burned bamboo in the yard.

It was dark. When the beast Nian broke into the village, its eyes were blinded by red. The crackling of firecrackers scared it away. Over time, the beast Nian would not come. However, lighting candles, wearing new clothes, setting off firecrackers, and other ceremonies have been preserved and gradually formed the current Chinese New Year.

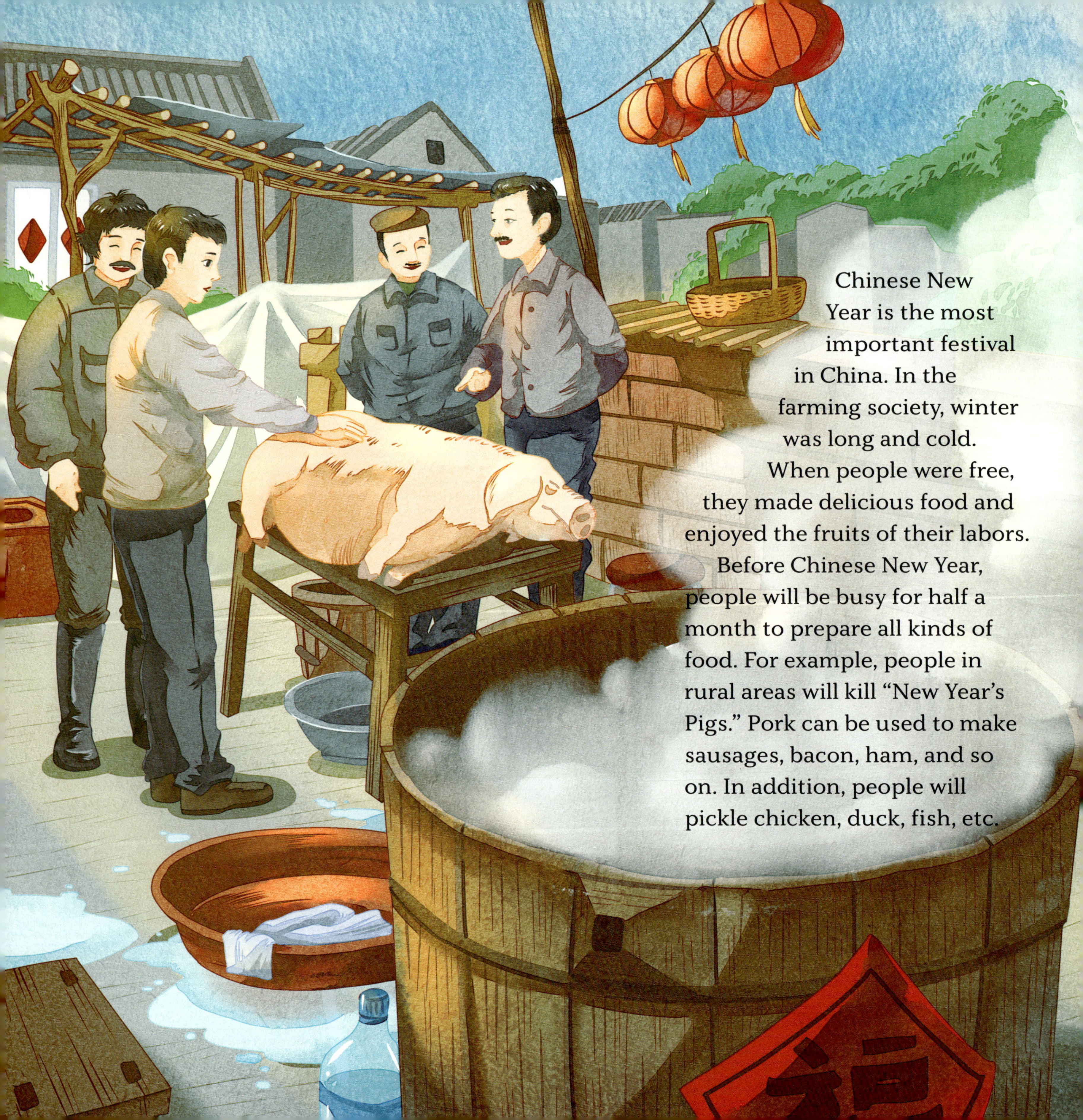

Chinese New Year is the most important festival in China. In the farming society, winter was long and cold. When people were free, they made delicious food and enjoyed the fruits of their labors. Before Chinese New Year, people will be busy for half a month to prepare all kinds of food. For example, people in rural areas will kill “New Year’s Pigs.” Pork can be used to make sausages, bacon, ham, and so on. In addition, people will pickle chicken, duck, fish, etc.

When Chinese New Year comes, each family should conduct a thorough cleanup, including the interior, exterior, front, and back of the house.

Special purchases for Chinese New Year should also be prepared in advance. Fried melon seeds, fried peanuts, fried Sanzi, fried meatballs, fried rice cakes ... There are special New Year goods in different places. Now, more and more people go directly to the market to buy ready-made New Year goods or order them directly online, which is both convenient and affordable.

On New Year's Eve, every household sticks New Year scrolls to pray for a good life in the new year.

Lunar New Year's Day

Wang Anshi

Amid the crackling firecrackers
a year did fly,
The spring breeze brings warm
and wine.
Over each household see the
sunshine,
Man would exchange the old
peachwood charm with the
fine.

Whisper to you

New Year scrolls have existed since ancient times and evolved from a kind of red mahogany plate called "Taofu."

Many people also stick "window flowers." The "window flower" is a kind of papercutting, which is mostly pasted on the window, so it is called the "window flower."

In addition to window flowers, people will also paste the character of "Fu" (福), New Year pictures, and "Guaqian," a paper-cutting pasted on the top of the door. Adults and children work together to decorate the house with festivity.

For kids, what is most exciting for Chinese New Year is setting off firecrackers besides pasting New Year scrolls and wearing new clothes.

On New Year's Eve, every household will set off firecrackers and fireworks. After the firecrackers are set off, the New Year's Eve dinner will begin.

Whisper to you

Firecracker has a history of more than 2,000 years in China. At first, people burned bamboo with fire. As it would make a "crackle" sound, people called it firecrackers. After the emergence of gunpowder, people filled the bamboo tube with gunpowder and made an "explosive firecracker." In the Song Dynasty (AD 960–1279), the folk began to use paper tubes and twine-wrapped gunpowder into strings to make "knitting guns," that is, "firecrackers."

Whisper to you

Generally speaking, there are 8–12 dishes for the New Year's Eve dinner. If the number of dishes is even, it means good things come in pairs. In the dinner, chicken, fish, meat, and eggs are necessary, but Chinese cuisine in different regions has its own characteristics. As a necessary dish, fish is normally not eaten but left for the next day, which means that it is more than sufficient every year.

Fireworks and firecrackers are crackling outside, and it is also bustling inside! The large family is getting together and having a "reunion dinner."

"Four Big Items" in Northeastern Region

They show the forthright style of the Northeast. It seems that this meal will not be authentic without any one of them.

Short Ribs

Pork Hock

Fish—more than sufficient every year

People from Suzhou will bury some water chestnuts in the rice and dig them out during the meal, which is called "Digging Yuanbao" (shoe-shaped gold ingot).

Chicken—big fortune and great profit

Crispy Meat with Clasping Bowl in Henan

This is the most common and popular dish on the table in Henan Province during Chinese New Year.

Four-Joy Meatballs
(braised pork balls in gravy sauce)

The four joys refer to “blessing, wealth, longevity, and happiness.”

Heqi in Anhui

This is the first dish of the New Year’s Eve dinner in Anhui Province, which means “peace, happiness, and harmony.”

Rice with Water Chestnuts in Suzhou

Fujian Hotpot

Steaming hot, with continuously added soup and ingredients, implies “the more you eat, the more you have, and the better your life will be.”

After a big New Year's Eve dinner, there comes the most expected part for kids: the seniors to give "lucky money." After the lucky money is distributed, the whole family will stay together to welcome the new year, which is called "Shou Sui" (waiting for the arrival of the New Year).

There is a story about Shou Sui. In ancient China, there was a kind of little monster called "Sui," who chose to touch the child's head, especially on New Year's Eve, and the child would get sick after being touched. The adults were afraid that the Sui would hurt the children, so they lit the lights all night and didn't sleep. That's where the tradition of "Shou Sui" came from.

The children couldn't stay up late, so when they fell asleep, the adults would wrap the copper money in red paper and put it under the children's pillows. When the little monster Sui was about to reach out and touch the child, a golden light came out of the pillow scaring the little monster to scream away. From then on, everyone followed suit. "岁" (sui), meaning "year" and "祟" (sui), the little monster, are homophones in Chinese, and the lucky money is called "Ya Sui" (oppress the monster Sui) money in Chinese. So children can spend a year in peace and security when they get the lucky money.

After the first cock crow, the new year begins. In the crackling sound of firecrackers, men and women, old and young, all get up early and wear new clothes to greet each other.

The children pay New Year's greetings to their elders first. Neighbors and friends meet to congratulate each other: "Happy New Year!" and "Happy New Year!"

Breakfast on the first day of Chinese New Year is different for people in the North and South. But they all share the same purpose: to wish the new year peaceful and auspicious!

People in most northern areas, such as the Northeastern Region and Shandong Province, eat dumplings on the first day, which means "good luck."

In some places in Guanzhong (Central Shannxi) and Henan Province, dumplings and noodles are cooked together, which is called "golden string through the ingot" or "silver thread hanging gourd."

Drinking chicken soup in Hubei Province symbolizes "safe and sound"; eating chicken feet means "grasping wealth in the new year"; eating the chicken head means "standing out."

In Hunan Province, people eat "Chinese New Year cakes" (rice cakes), which means "one year is better than another."

Guangxi people eat sweet rice dumplings, which indicates that the new year will be sweet and pleasant, and people will have a harvest.

Minnan people in Fujian Province eat noodles for the first meal of Chinese New Year, which means "for long."

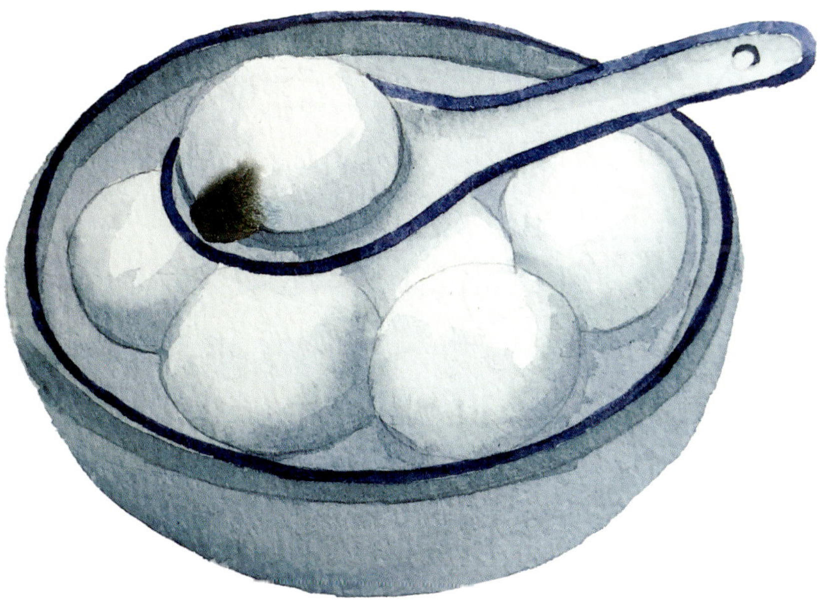

People in Shanghai eat Tangyuan (glutinous rice balls), which means "perfection" in the new year, and the soup is indispensable, which means "rich and powerful."

In Haikou, people have to practice abstinence from meat on the first day, which is intended to pray for longevity and bring purity and peace throughout the year.

On the second day, most regions of China have the custom of visiting their parents' homes. Mom and Dad will take the children to visit Grandma's house with gifts to pay New Year's greetings.

Grandparents have already been waiting at the door happily!

After the New Year's greetings, they will have a reunion lunch together at noon and talk about the fun of the year.

On the third and fourth days, people began to walk around. After breakfast, the whole family began to visit relatives. When they meet, they say to each other: "Wish you prosperity" and "Happy New Year," and all of them are smiling. In some places, people don't visit relatives on the third day, so they can get up later to make up for sleep.

There are many folk customs and taboos from the first to the fifth day of Chinese New Year, such as not cooking with raw rice, not taking needles and threads, not dumping garbage, not breaking things, etc. After the fifth day, these taboos are lifted, so this day is called “Po Wu” (breaking five).

People in rural areas will sweep kitchen ashes and garbage outside the door and set off firecrackers on the fifth day. This is called “Song Qiong,” which means sending poverty away and ushering in prosperity and happiness in the new year.

The seventh day is called the "Renri Festival," also known as People Day. It is said that Nü Wa (a goddess in Chinese mythology) created humans on the seventh day after creating animals such as chickens, dogs, pigs, cows, and horses, so this day is a festival for humanity.

Whisper to you

"Renri Festival" is an ancient festival with a history of at least 2,000 years in China. On this day, some regions have the custom of eating "Qi Bao Geng" (seven-treasure soup), which is made of seven fresh seasonal vegetables and rice noodles. In addition, some places still have the custom of eating noodles on this day, which means wealth and longevity.

Row-Boat Dance

During Chinese New Year, various interesting activities are carried out throughout the country.

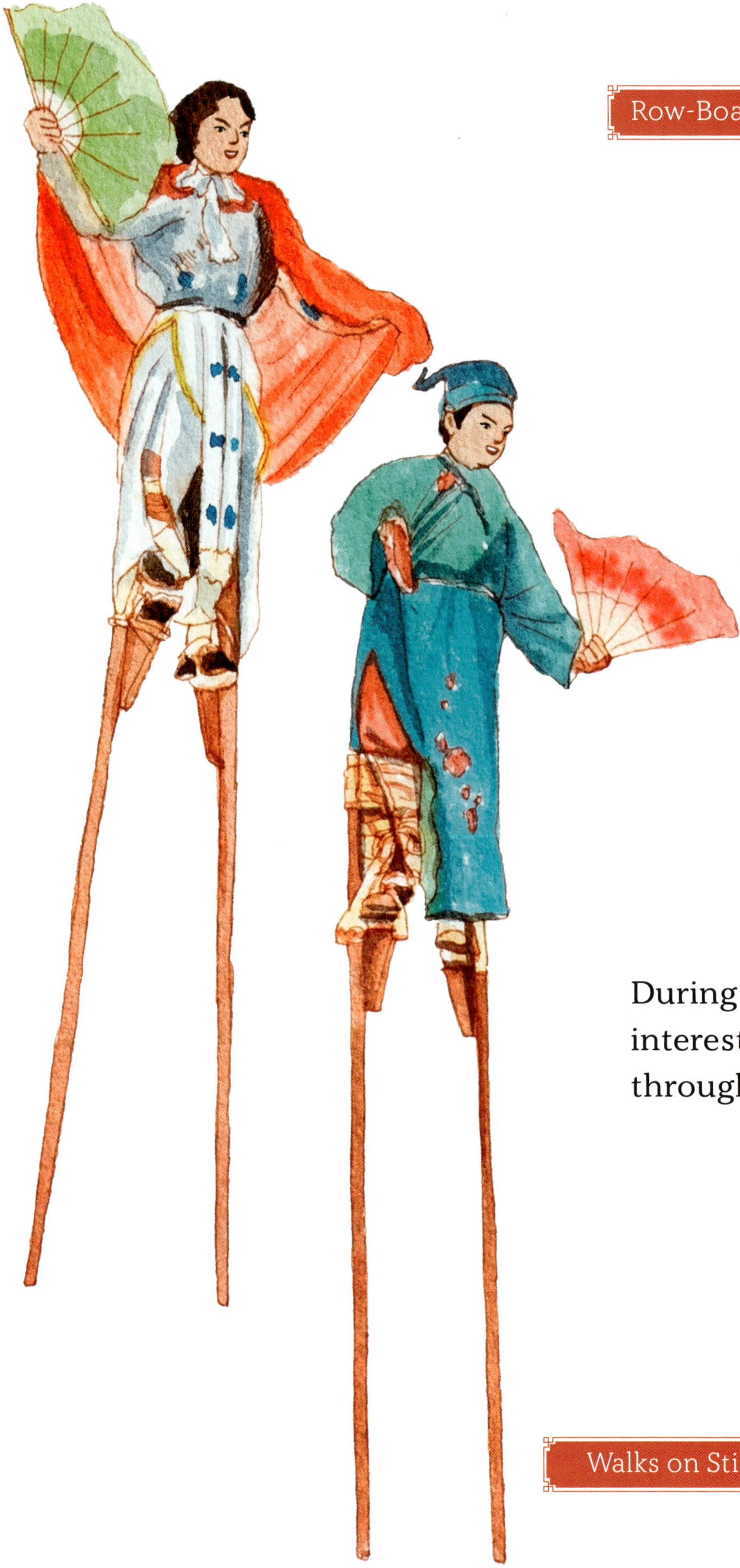

Walks on Stilts in Northeast China

地坛春节文化庙会
Beijing Temple Fair
文明
入场

Gansu Taiping Drum

Shaanxi Yangge and Waist Drum

Dragon and Lion Dance in the South

Tujia Nationality Waving Dance

The fifteenth day is the first full moon night of the year. People call it the Lantern Festival, also known as the Shangyuan Festival.

Throughout the country, there are customs such as appreciating lanterns, guessing riddles posted on lanterns, and performing dragon dances. Some areas in the South will also release Kongming lanterns (a sky lantern made of paper) to celebrate the Lantern Festival.

The Lantern Festival also has specific food. On this day, people in the North usually eat Yuanxiao (rice glue balls), while in the South, they usually eat Tangyuan (another kind of glutinous rice balls).

The end of the Lantern Festival also means the end of Chinese New Year, and the celebration of Chinese New Year is basically over, but people's love and yearning for the festival always exist.

Whisper to you

The difference between Yuanxiao and Tangyuan:

To make Yuanxiao, you need to mix the filling, rub it into small pieces, drain and rinse, and then throw it into a bowl full of glutinous rice flour to roll, and repeat several times until it rolls into a ball shape. After cooking, the soup will be rather thick, like glutinous rice porridge. Tangyuan requires one to grab a small ball of wetted dough and extrude it into a wafer shape, pick a ball of filling and squeeze it into the glutinous rice slices, and then rub it with both hands to seal it completely.

Chinese New Year is celebrated not only by people in China but also by many overseas Chinese. Nations in East and Southeast Asia affected by Chinese cultures, such as the Republic of Korea, Japan, the Socialist Republic of Viet Nam, Malaysia, etc., celebrate Chinese New Year as well.

As international communication between China and other countries becomes frequent, Chinese New Year has become more and more influential and has gradually become a worldwide festival. Nearly twenty countries and regions, including the United States of America, Canada, and the Republic of Mauritius, have designated Chinese New Year as a legal holiday in the whole nation or in some cities under their jurisdiction.

熙春
闻
歲全家共慶
清
乾坤
年年好
琢磨多
雲山
步步高
意
福
才高

CHINESE FESTIVALS

Chinese New Year

Edited by Li Chaodong
Translated by Joanna Jiayan Zhang and Vivian Qinwen Yan

First published in 2023 by Royal Collins Publishing Group Inc.
Groupe Publication Royal Collins Inc.
BKM Royalcollins Publishers Private Limited

Headquarters: 550-555 boul. René-Lévesque O Montréal (Québec) H2Z1B1 Canada
India office: 805 Hemkunt House, 8th Floor, Rajendra Place, New Delhi 110 008

ISBN: 978-1-4878-1151-8

To find out more about our publications, please visit www.royalcollins.com.

ABOUT THE EDITOR

Li Chaodong, born in 1963, graduated from the Department of History of East China Normal University. He is a famous education publisher in China. He has edited and published more than 50 sets of books. He has won the title of "National Leading Talent in Press and Publication" and "China's Annual Publication Figure." He is the Founding Vice President of the All-China Federation of Industry and Commerce Book Industry Chamber of Commerce, Vice President of the Fifth Council of the Books and Periodicals Distribution Association of China, Vice Chairman of Anhui Publishing Association, and Vice Chairman of Jiangsu Publishing Association.